Pocahontas

By Laura L. Sullivan

New York

Published in 2021 by Cavendish Square Publishing, LLC
243 5th Avenue, Suite 136, New York, NY 10016

First Edition

Website: cavendishsq.com

Library of Congress Cataloging-in-Publication Data

Names: Sullivan, Laura L, author.
Title: Pocahontas / Laura L Sullivan.
Description: First edition. | New York, NY : Cavendish Square Publishing, 2021. | Series: The inside guide: famous Native Americans | Includes index.
Identifiers: LCCN 2019047181 (print) | LCCN 2019047182 (ebook) | ISBN 9781502651266 (library binding) | ISBN 9781502651242 (paperback) | ISBN 9781502651259 (set) | ISBN 9781502651273 (ebook)
Subjects: LCSH: Pocahontas, -1617–Juvenile literature. | Powhatan Indians–Biography–Juvenile literature.
Classification: LCC E99.P85 S85 2021 (print) | LCC E99.P85 (ebook) | DDC 975.501092 [B]–dc23
LC record available at https://lccn.loc.gov/2019047181
LC ebook record available at https://lccn.loc.gov/2019047182

Editor: Kristen Susienka
Copy Editor: Rebecca Rohan
Designer: Deanna Paternostro

The photographs in this book are used by permission and through the courtesy of: Cover Three Lions/Getty Images; p. 4 Colin McConnell/Toronto Star via Getty Images; p. 6 Print Collector/Getty Images; p. 7 Photo12/Universal Images Group via Getty Images; pp. 8, 29 (top right) Interim Archives/Getty Images; p. 10 Historic Collection/Alamy Stock Photo; pp. 12, 24 Everett Historical/Shutterstock.com; p. 13 Joe Sohm/Visions of America/Universal Images Group via Getty Images; p. 14 MPI/Getty Images; pp. 15, 18, 22, 29 (bottom right) North Wind Picture Archives/Alamy Stock Photo; p. 16 Adrin Snider/Newport News Daily Press/Tribune News Service via Getty Images; p. 19 Hulton Archive/Getty Images; p. 20 Glasshouse Images/Alamy Stock Photo; p. 21 Dennis Tarnay, Jr./Alamy Stock Photo; p. 25 History and Art Collection/Alamy Stock Photo; p. 26 Regine Poirier/Shutterstock.com; p. 27 Entertainment Pictures/Alamy Stock Photo; p. 28 (top left) morgan hill/Alamy Stock Photo; pp. 28 (top right), 29 (left) Universal History Archive/Universal Images Group via Getty Images; p. 28 (bottom left) dbimages/Alamy Stock Photo; p. 28 (bottom right) Keam Collection/Getty Images.

Printed in the United States of America

CONTENTS

A group's stories are a big part of its identity. Here, Native American artist Saul Williams explains how legends influenced his painting.

FROM STORY TO HISTORY

Around the world, legends help people learn about a **culture** or country. They help others understand an area's beliefs, traditions, values, or past. They teach people lessons or help them remember a part of history better. There are many famous legends from all around the world, including Native American cultures. Native American communities have lived in what's now the United States for thousands of years. Each community has incredible legends. Sometimes the legends are invented. Others are based on real events or people.

The legends about real people might include different stories about the same person, or events in a person's life might be remembered differently in each story. Small details like what was said or done might be lost to time, so people have to imagine what a conversation or action was like. However, historians work to find the truth behind the legend so people get to learn the real stories about men and women who are remembered in history.

Fast Fact

The oldest written legend is *The Epic of Gilgamesh.* It was written in 2000 BCE.

Fast Fact

Pocahontas's father was chief of 30 tribes.

This painting of the famous Pocahontas was done in 1937. It's based on stories about her.

A Woman of Legend

One familiar American legend is about a Native American woman named Pocahontas. Much of what we know about her was written by an English settler named John Smith. He arrived in the colony of Virginia in 1607 and met Pocahontas and her father many times.

Pocahontas was the daughter of a Native American chief and lived in the 1600s, when America looked very different than it does today. There were no big cities or highways in Pocahontas's world. Planes, trains, and cars weren't around yet either.

Native Americans like Pocahontas lived in communities called villages. They often lived in houses they built from the trees around them. They grew corn and other crops that kept their families and friends fed

This image shows what Native American villages in the colony of Virginia looked like when white settlers arrived in the 1600s.

JAMESTOWN, VIRGINIA

In the early 1600s, many nations in Europe were looking to America for places to explore and settle. The Spanish had been exploring parts of what was called the New World since the 1400s. France was also settling parts of what are now Canada and the northern United States. England decided to set up colonies across the ocean too. They named these colonies after places or people back home.

In 1607, the English started the colony of Virginia. It was named for Queen Elizabeth I, who was also called the Virgin Queen. The first settlement in Virginia was Jamestown. John Smith was one of the people who started Jamestown. Back then, the settlers worked hard to build places in which they could live. They faced harsh winters and survived. Today, Jamestown still exists. It has museums and a historic village to remember Virginia's history.

This drawing imagines what Jamestown looked like in the 1600s.

Fast Fact

Pocahontas belonged to part of the Powhatan empire. Her main tribe was called the Pamunkey tribe. They lived in Virginia.

and that they could sometimes trade with others. Warriors protected the community. Each village had its own leaders. When Europeans arrived, they called the leaders chiefs.

People most remember Pocahontas for her friendship with John Smith. Smith wrote down stories of his meetings with Pocahontas, and those stories have been retold many times by many people. Today, her story is one of the best-known Native American tales. However, Pocahontas is just one of many Native Americans whose story helped shape the history of the United States.

Pocahontas's story has become an American legend today, but what was Pocahontas's life really like? Read on to find out!

Although stories sometimes show her as older, Pocahontas was a young child when she first met the English.

"LITTLE PLAYFUL ONE"

Pocahontas was born around 1596 near what's now Jamestown, Virginia. Like many Native Americans, she had several names. One was Amonute. This was the name she received when she was born. Another name was more private: Matoaka. Most often, though, she was called Pocahontas. It's a nickname that means "little playful one." Historians think she got this nickname because she seemed to always be happy and asked a lot of questions.

The Chief's Daughter

Pocahontas was the daughter of a man commonly known as Powhatan. His real name was Wahunsenacah. He was called Powhatan because he led the Powhatan empire. The English called him the Powhatan, which meant "the chief." He was the paramount, or main, chief of a group of tribes that was also called the Powhatan. The Powhatan tribes formed an empire. It stretched across much of what is now the US state of Virginia. The tribes fought wars together, and each chief in the tribe listened to Powhatan's advice. He was the ruler of the empire.

Fast Fact

Another meaning for Pocahontas is "badly behaved child."

Not a lot is known about Pocahontas's mother. She either died or went back to live with her own tribe after Pocahontas was born. Powhatan had many children, but people believe Pocahontas was his favorite. He would do anything for her.

Fast Fact

Playful Pocahontas spent time with the settlers' children. She even did cartwheels with them!

Settlers

In 1607, about 100 settlers arrived in Powhatan's territory. They had traveled across the ocean from England. The settlers were all working for a company called the Virginia Company. Its main mission was to send its workers overseas to set up new towns in America. The first settlers in Virginia named the colony and built a fort to live in and to keep out Native Americans who might hurt them.

Most of the Native Americans they met were part of Powhatan's tribe. Not everyone liked the English in Powhatan's territory. Powhatan himself was unsure about them.

John Smith

The most famous English settler from that time was John Smith. He had fought in wars in Europe, had been captured in battle, and had escaped. He also knew a lot about surviving in difficult conditions. He'd decided to join the Virginia Company and become a founding member of Jamestown.

While in Virginia, Smith took detailed notes and wrote about what he saw. He also traded with some of Powhatan's people. One day, he and a group of explorers were on the

John Smith played a big part in Pocahontas's story.

Chickahominy River when they were **ambushed**. The people who'd attacked were Powhatan's relatives.

Saving John Smith

According to legend, Powhatan wanted to kill Smith. He made him put his head on a rock and was about to smash his head with a club. Just then, the young Pocahontas ran up. She put her head between Smith's head and the club. The attack stopped. Pocahontas had saved Smith's life.

In some Native American **oral histories**, though, Smith's life was never in danger. Instead, it was all part of an adoption ceremony. Smith just didn't understand what was going on. The story of Pocahontas saving his life was how he came to understand the events. He wrote the story down in his journal years after it happened.

No matter why the attack took place, after that day, Smith was thought of by the Native Americans as part of the Powhatan tribe.

Friendship, Then Conflict

For a few years, the settlers and the tribe got along. Powhatan sent the settlers many gifts of food. He thought if he kept the settlers happy, they would help him if a different tribe attacked his empire.

Shown here are people dressed in the clothes English settlers wore at the time of John Smith and Pocahontas.

This painting imagines what it was like when the settlers arrived in Virginia.

Pocahontas often visited the settlers. The settlers knew she was Powhatan's favorite. She taught John Smith about her language, and he taught her about his. They formed a friendship.

Later, though, Powhatan's people began to run out of food. They couldn't give the settlers any more, so the settlers threatened them. They said they would burn the Native American villages. After that, Powhatan moved his people farther away and didn't trade much with the settlers.

Marriage and Peace

In 1613, the settlers decided to capture Pocahontas. They thought this could force Powhatan to trade with them again. Powhatan paid a big **ransom**, but the settlers didn't let her go. Pocahontas eventually changed her name to Rebecca and married a settler named John Rolfe. However, Pocahontas had been married before, to a Powhatan man named Kocoum. They had a daughter named Ka-Okee. Rumors said Kocoum had been killed by the English after Pocahontas was kidnapped.

The marriage between Pocahontas and John Rolfe brought peace between the settlers and Powhatan's tribe. Pocahontas and John Rolfe later had a son named Thomas.

In 1616, Pocahontas and her husband and child traveled to England. She was very popular there. In 1617, she was about to return home when she became sick. She died of an unknown disease and was buried in England.

Fast Fact

Pocahontas and John Rolfe's son Thomas was left behind in England after Pocahontas died. John Rolfe returned to Virginia without him.

GROWING UP IN THE POWHATAN TRIBE

In Powhatan society, everything was inherited through the mother. For example, Pocahontas's father inherited several tribes from his mother. Therefore, women and girls were very important to their way of life.

Powhatan women did a lot for their families and communities. They learned how to build houses with woven mats over bent saplings. They could also farm, cook, prepare skins and furs, make baskets, and find **edible** wild plants. As a child, Pocahontas would have learned all of these things. She would have also shaved most of her hair with a sharp mussel shell. She wouldn't have worn many clothes in the summer. When she entered adulthood, around age 13, she would have grown her hair out and worn different clothing. Then, she was considered old enough to get married.

This map shows where different Native American communities lived in the United States in around 1700. The Powhatan homeland can be seen on this map.

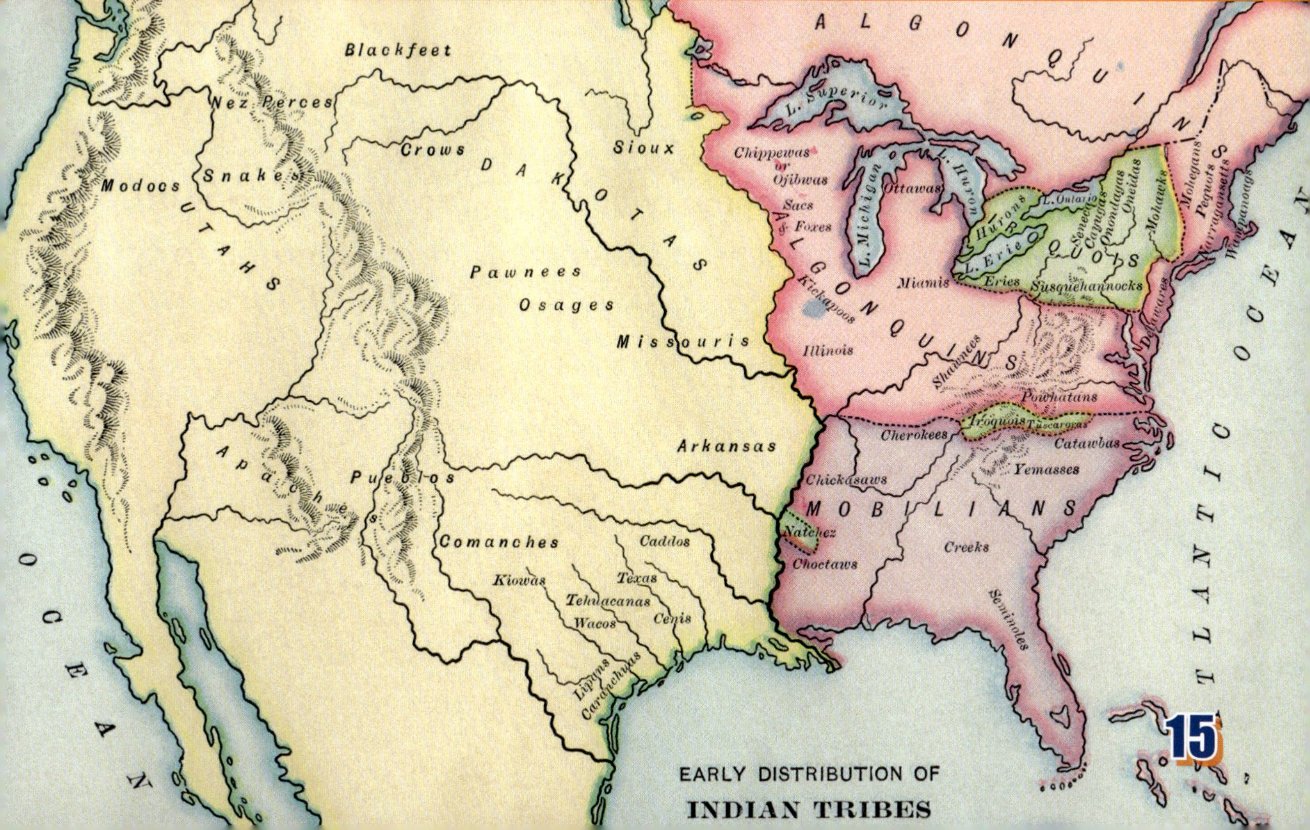

English colonists arrived in 1607 aboard three ships, models of which are seen here.

HELP IN THE NEW WORLD

In the 16th and 17th centuries, English people started to colonize America. Spain, France, and Portugal had started sending people to the New World much earlier. England wanted to catch up. King James I was the ruler of England who allowed the Virginia Company to form. The company's plan was to sail to the New World and start settlements there. It would also be the company that changed Pocahontas's life.

The English

In May 1607, three English ships arrived in the Chesapeake area of Virginia. They were called the *Susan Constant*, the *Godspeed*, and the *Discovery*. No doubt the giant sails and strange voices of the men on board alarmed the Native Americans who saw the ships. Maybe Pocahontas was one of them! As the settlers learned about the land, they decided that a fort was needed to protect them from the Native Americans.

Fast Fact

Jamestown was known as James Fort, James Towne, and James Citie at different points of its early history.

The settlers explored their surroundings and chose a spot about 40 miles (64 kilometers) inland, along a river, to build their fort. They thought the river location would be easy to

John Smith met with the Powhatan people many times to help the settlers in Jamestown.

defend and was a good place for ships to move, or transport, people and supplies. The fort was triangular and had a church, kitchen, houses, and buildings where meetings or business were conducted. The goal of the colony was to make a lot of money and send goods back to England.

Hardship and Help

The settlers soon found that living away from England was difficult. Winters were harsh. There were droughts during the summer. People starved. They also faced being attacked by Native Americans. Because of these problems, many early colonists died. Lack of food was the main killer. In fact, everyone might have died if Powhatan had not given the colonists food. He and his people, including Pocahontas, also gave them advice about how to survive.

Later, other ships brought more settlers and supplies to help the fort and the colony continue. It was with Pocahontas's help that relations between settlers and her people were friendly rather than hostile for a period of time.

Fast Fact

Pocahontas and her tribe called the area in which they lived Tsenacommacah. It meant "a land with lots of people."

Settlers made fortunes growing tobacco.

The New Money Crop

One way the Powhatan helped the settlers was by showing them how to farm **tobacco**, which is a plant found in the Americas. Tobacco first came to Europe in 1559. People thought it protected them from sickness. Tobacco was one of the reasons the colonists wanted to start businesses in Virginia. If people could grow enough of it, they could send it back to England and make a lot of money. Many Native American tribes also used tobacco, including the Powhatan. John Rolfe, Pocahontas's English husband, learned from the Powhatan how to farm tobacco in a different way that was very successful. With the Powhatan's help, he started big tobacco farms in Virginia.

Going to England

Pocahontas played a major role in helping settlers and the Powhatan live in peace. Not only did she visit the Virginia fort often, but she also got

This image imagines what Pocahontas's father, Powhatan, looked like.

to know John Smith well. Later, her marriage to John Rolfe bridged a gap between settlers and her people. It also gave her the opportunity to travel and be an **ambassador** for her people.

In 1616, Pocahontas visited England with her husband and their son, Thomas. While she was there, she got to meet England's king and queen, King James I and Queen Anne. Everyone was interested in Pocahontas. Many had never met a Native American before. They called her a princess. They treated her well—possibly because she acted like a European, and they believed she had been "tamed."

Months after she had arrived in England, Pocahontas met John Smith again. She thought he had died. Seeing him made her angry and sad. She told him she wasn't happy with the way the English treated her people.

The peace Pocahontas helped bring to her people and the English settlers didn't last long. In the centuries ahead, life changed even more for Native Americans. In the 1800s, many Native Americans were forced from their homes. They couldn't live their traditional lifestyles. This happened all over the country and hurt many Native Americans. It changed their ways of life. It also forced them onto reservations, where many live today.

Fast Fact

The conversation John Smith and Pocahontas had in England was their last before Pocahontas died.

THE PAMUNKEY

Pocahontas was born into the Pamunkey tribe, which was part of the Powhatan empire. Her descendants, or relatives, today are still members of the Pamunkey. The Pamunkey continue carrying on their traditions and celebrating their heritage. They can be found in King William, Virginia, on the Pamunkey Reservation. Visitors to the reservation can visit the Pamunkey Museum and Cultural Center, which records the tribe's proud history. The tribe has been officially recognized by the US government since January 2016.

For a long time, the Pamunkey didn't consider Pocahontas a celebrated ancestor. It was only after the popular animated movie about her life—titled *Pocahontas*—came out in the 1990s that the Pamunkey started to celebrate Pocahontas's legacy.

This sign welcomes people to the Pamunkey Reservation today.

This drawing shows the scene in which Pocahontas saves John Smith's life. No one knows if it actually happened.

POCAHONTAS: MYTH AND REALITY

Most people think of Pocahontas's story as very exciting. The most popular part of her story today is her relationship with John Smith. Tales about the two of them are based on a story John Smith wrote many years after he met Pocahontas. Some people reading the story think John Smith and Pocahontas loved each other. No one knows for sure, but it's unlikely that story is true. John Smith was much older than Pocahontas. In fact, Pocahontas was only 10 or 11 years old when she met Smith. It's important to remember that some stories about Pocahontas are more legend than truth.

Pocahontas and John Smith

Fast Fact
Pocahontas was the first Native American to be on a postage stamp, in 1907.

The idea of romantic love between Pocahontas and John Smith first appeared because of Smith's story about Pocahontas saving his life. Some people think she stepped in to save him because she loved him. However, the first two times Smith told the story of his capture, he didn't mention Pocahontas saving him. He didn't tell that story until much later. When he did tell it, he was writing to Queen Anne right before Pocahontas visited

England. He might have wanted to make Pocahontas and himself seem more interesting.

There are also stories about Pocahontas saving other settlers. One story is about two young settlers who were living with the Powhatans to learn more about how they lived. That was normal for the young boys from Virginia and Powhatan's empire to do. When they ran away, the chief was going to kill them. Stories say Pocahontas helped one of the boys get to safety.

Fast Fact

Pocahontas became a follower of the Christian religion. She changed her name to Rebecca when she became a Christian.

A Love Story?

Pocahontas's interactions with settlers continued after she saved John Smith and the boy settlers too. After her capture, Pocahontas married John Rolfe. Rolfe had arrived in Virginia in 1610. He was a farmer who grew tobacco. He had much success growing and selling sweeter West Indian tobacco to English people. It helped Virginia's economy.

Some stories say Pocahontas fell in love with Rolfe. However, the oral history of the Mattaponi tribe (once a part of Powhatan's empire) tells a different story. They say Pocahontas was forced to marry Rolfe.

She had been captured by the English in 1613 and was living in Jamestown at that time. If she didn't marry Rolfe,

John Rolfe was a farmer in Virginia who later married Pocahontas.

Pocahontas learned English ways after marrying John Rolfe. This painting shows her meeting King James in England.

she might never have been freed. She also knew that the settlers were burning her people's villages and killing the Powhatan people. Rumors said they had killed Kocoum too. When peace talks didn't go well at first, Pocahontas announced that she would marry Rolfe. Her father granted his permission, which allowed her to marry Rolfe. After that, things got better between the settlers and the Native Americans. She might have married Rolfe to help her people.

Rolfe knew that if he was related to the tribes by marriage, he could make better deals with them. Both Pocahontas and Rolfe had things to gain by marrying each other.

Peace Brings More Settlers

Some of these stories about Pocahontas and her people were probably told to make it look like Virginia was a safe place to live. If English people felt that way, more of them would want to move there and make money for the colony. In 1616, Pocahontas and her family made a trip across the

This statue in Jamestown helps people remember Pocahontas today.

ocean to England. The English people loved her. She met many important people, including the king and queen.

Pocahontas's visit to England helped convince some people that Native Americans weren't a threat. The period of peace between the Powhatan people and the English during Pocahontas's marriage was called the Peace of Pocahontas. That peace encouraged more people to move to the New World. However, this also meant that the Powhatan were pushed out of their homes faster.

Her Story

Pocahontas never got to tell her story. Most of the information about her comes from John Smith. He was known for making up stories. In fact, he once claimed another "princess" also saved his life!

Today, many people see Pocahontas as a **role model**. She was a young woman trying to do what was best for her people. She became a symbol of good relations between the settlers and Native Americans. Her legend continues to bridge cultures. Her place in Native American and US history will last as long as her story keeps being told.

Fast Fact

Native American actress Irene Bedard voiced the character of Pocahontas in the Disney movie. She has played many Native American characters in her career.

DISNEY'S POCAHONTAS

Many people know the story of Pocahontas from the 1995 Disney movie *Pocahontas.* The movie was groundbreaking in many ways. It was the first time a woman of color was the star of a Disney animated movie. Pocahontas was the first Native American Disney princess. The movie brought her story to millions of children and their families. It also led to a sequel, *Pocahontas II: Journey to a New World*, which came out in 1998. It followed Pocahontas on her trip to England and her reunion with John Smith.

However, the movies about Pocahontas didn't represent her as she truly was. The first movie made her much older when she met John Smith. Both movies also made it seem like she and Smith were in love. The first film also didn't represent the Powhatan culture very well. Still, because of these movies, people became more aware of Pocahontas and Native American history in general.

Many people know about Pocahontas because of the Disney movie about her life.

THINK ABOUT IT!

Use these questions to help you think more deeply about this topic.

1. Imagine growing up in Pocahontas's village. What would you see? What would you do?

2. How old was Pocahontas when she met John Smith? How does knowing her real age change your understanding of her story?

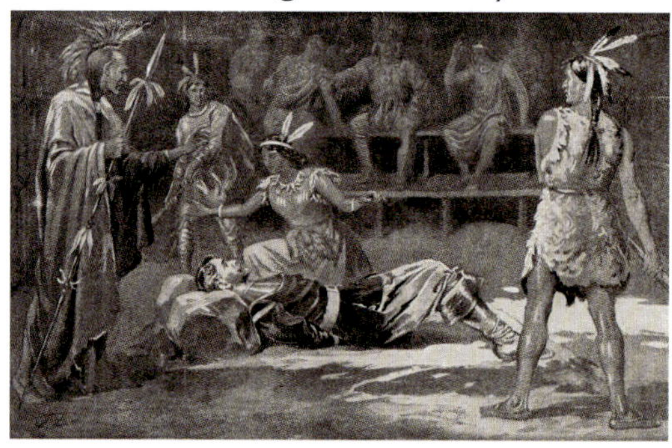

3. What are some differences between popular legends about Pocahontas and what might really have happened in her life? Why is it important to know where we get our information from about her life?

4. In what ways is Pocahontas remembered today?

TIMELINE

Pocahontas's Life

1596
Pocahontas is born.

1607
Pocahontas first meets John Smith.

1613
Pocahontas is captured by colonists.

1614
Pocahontas marries John Rolfe.

1616
Pocahontas, John Rolfe, and their son Thomas travel to England.

1617
Pocahontas dies.

World Events

1607
Colonists land in Virginia.

1610–1614
The first Anglo-Powhatan War, fought between English settlers and Native Americans, takes place.

1612
The first tobacco is harvested in Virginia.

1618
Powhatan dies, and his brother takes over.

1622–1632
The second Anglo-Powhatan War is fought.

GLOSSARY

ambassador: A person who speaks well of a country, travels on a country's behalf, and encourages other countries to make partnerships with them.

ambush: To sneak up on and attack.

culture: A group of people's way of life, beliefs, traditions, religious practices, or stories.

edible: Able to be eaten; not poisonous.

oral history: Information about a group of people, such as stories, that is passed down through speaking.

ransom: Payment made in exchange for a person who has been kidnapped or taken prisoner.

role model: Someone who others look up to as an example of a good person or leader.

tobacco: A plant containing the drug nicotine, which is dried and smoked.